MASSACHUSETTS

The Bay State

BY
JOHN HAMILTON

Abdo & Daughters

An imprint of Abdo Publishing | abdopublishing.com

abdopublishing.com

Published by ABDO Publishing, a division of ABDO, PO Box 398166, Minneapolis, Minnesota 55439. Copyright © 2017 by Abdo Consulting Group, Inc. International copyrights reserved in all countries. No part of this book may be reproduced in any form without written permission from the publisher. ABDO & Daughters™ is a trademark and logo of ABDO Publishing.

Printed in the United States of America, North Mankato, Minnesota.
022016
092016

THIS BOOK CONTAINS
RECYCLED MATERIALS

Editor: Sue Hamilton   **Contributing Editor:** Bridget O'Brien
Graphic Design: Sue Hamilton
Cover Art Direction: Candice Keimig   **Cover Photo Selection:** Neil Klinepier
Cover Photo: iStock
Interior Images: Alamy, Albert Bierstadt, AP, Boston Bruins, Boston Celtics, Boston Red Sox, Bull Brook Paleo Archeology Site, Corbis, Dreamstime, Getty, Granger, Harvard University, History in Full Color-Restoration/Colorization, International Volleyball Hall of Fame, iStock, John Hamilton, Ken Bohrer, Library of Congress, Massachusetts Secretary of the Commonwealth, Mile High Maps, Minden Pictures, Mountain High Maps, National Archives and Records, National Gallery of Art/Gilbert Stuart, New England Patriots, New England Revolution, New York Public Library, One Mile Up, White House, Wikimedia, Zoo New England.

Statistics: *State and City Populations*, U.S. Census Bureau, July 1, 2015/2014 estimates; *Land and Water Area*, U.S. Census Bureau, 2010 Census, MAF/TIGER database; *State Temperature Extremes*, NOAA National Climatic Data Center; *Climatology and Average Annual Precipitation*, NOAA National Climatic Data Center, 1980-2015 statewide averages; *State Highest and Lowest Points*, NOAA National Geodetic Survey.

Websites: To learn more about the United States, visit booklinks.abdopublishing.com. These links are routinely monitored and updated to provide the most current information available.

Cataloging-in-Publication Data

Names: Hamilton, John, 1959- author.
Title: Massachusetts / by John Hamilton.
Description: Minneapolis, MN : Abdo Publishing, [2017] | Series: The United
    States of America | Includes index.
Identifiers: LCCN 2015957614 | ISBN 9781680783230 (lib. bdg.) |
    ISBN 9781680774276 (ebook)
Subjects: LCSH: Massachusetts--Juvenile literature.
Classification: DDC 974.4--dc23
LC record available at http://lccn.loc.gov/2015957614

CONTENTS

THE
BAY
STATE

Massachusetts is called the "Cradle of Liberty." It is a place rich in history. The Pilgrims came ashore in 1620 and later celebrated the first Thanksgiving. In 1775, the "shot heard 'round the world" at the Battles of Lexington and Concord marked the beginning of the American Revolution.

Massachusetts has always been full of big ideas, despite its small size. Many top universities, museums, and high-tech companies are found in Massachusetts, especially in the bustling Boston area. There is natural beauty in every corner of the state, from sandy beaches to forested mountains. And to the delight of food lovers, Massachusetts is the home of Boston cream pie.

Massachusetts is nicknamed "The Bay State," thanks to scenic Cape Cod Bay, where the first Europeans settled. People who live in Massachusetts today are often called Bay Staters.

Nobska Point Light sits on the southwestern tip of Cape Cod Bay, Massachusetts.

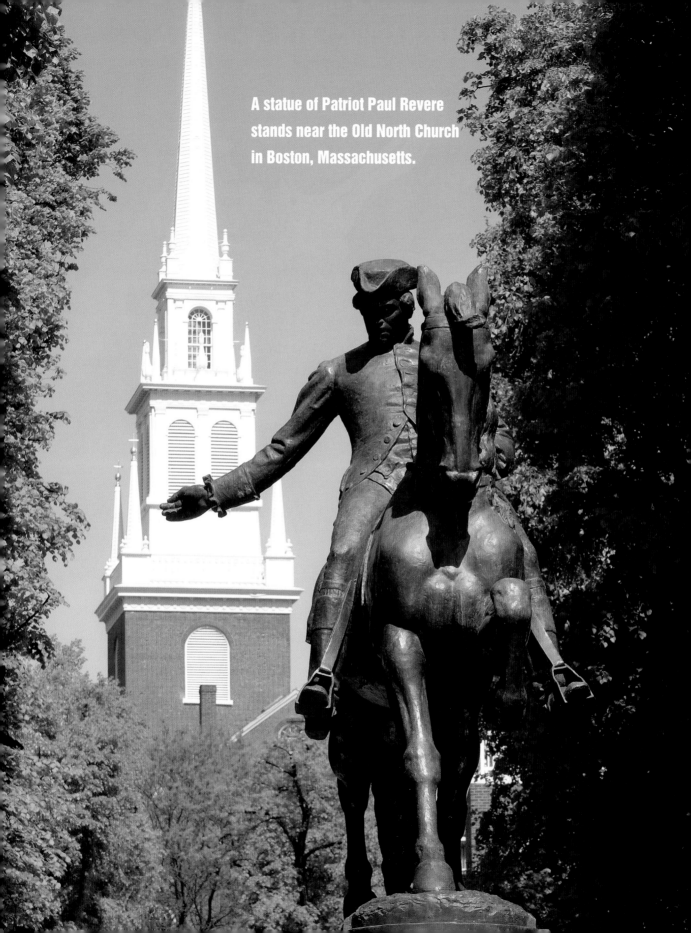

A statue of Patriot Paul Revere stands near the Old North Church in Boston, Massachusetts.

QUICK FACTS

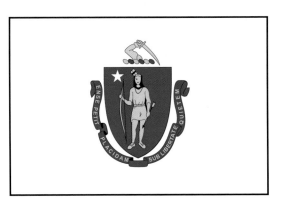

Name: Massachusetts comes from the name of an Algonquian-speaking tribe of Native Americans called the Massachuset. The word probably means "people of the great hills."

State Capital: Boston, population 655,884

Date of Statehood: February 6, 1788 (6th state)

Population: 6,794,422 (14th-most populous state)

Area (Total Land and Water): 10,554 square miles (27,335 sq km), 44th-largest state

Largest City: Boston, population 655,884

Nickname: The Bay State

Motto: *Ense petit placidam sub libertate quietem* (By the sword we seek peace, but peace only under liberty)

State Bird: Black-Capped Chickadee

State Flower: Mayflower

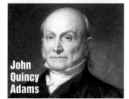

State Gemstone: Rhodonite

State Tree: American Elm

State Song: "All Hail to Massachusetts"

Highest Point: Mount Greylock, 3,491 feet (1,064 m)

Lowest Point: Atlantic Ocean, 0 feet (0 m)

Average July High Temperature: 81°F (27°C)

Record High Temperature: 107°F (42°C), in Chester and New Bedford on August 2, 1975

Average January Low Temperature: 16°F (-9°C)

Record Low Temperature: -35°F (-37°C), in Chester on January 12, 1981

Average Annual Precipitation: 48 inches (122 cm)

Number of U.S. Senators: 2

Number of U.S. Representatives: 9

U.S. Presidents Born in Massachusetts: John Adams, John Quincy Adams, John F. Kennedy, George H.W. Bush

U.S. Postal Service Abbreviation: MA

GEOGRAPHY

Massachusetts is part of a six-state region called New England, in the northeastern part of the United States. The state's total land area is 10,554 square miles (27,335 sq km), making it the 6th-smallest state. Despite its size, it has several distinct regions.

Along Massachusetts's western border with New York is the Taconic Range. Mount Greylock rises up 3,491 feet (1,064 m) here, the highest point in the state. East of the Taconic Range are the Berkshire Mountains. They are often called the Berkshire Hills, or simply "The Berkshires." These steeply rolling mountains run north and south, occupying most of far-western Massachusetts. The Taconic Range and Berkshire Mountains are part of the Appalachian Mountains. The area's rural charm, woods, and lakes attract nature lovers. There are many resorts and performing arts centers.

The beautiful Berkshire Mountains are a popular vacation area.

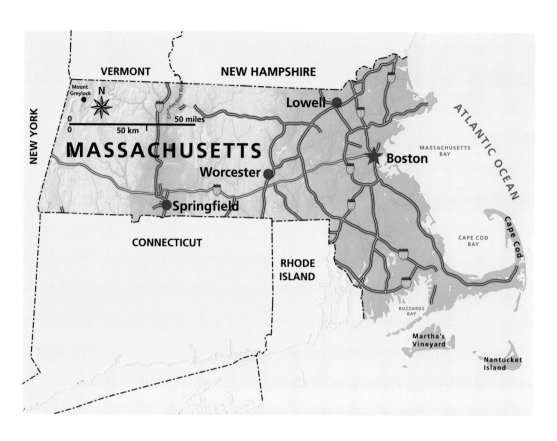

Massachusetts's total land and water area is 10,554 square miles (27,335 sq km). It is the 44th-largest state. The state capital is Boston.

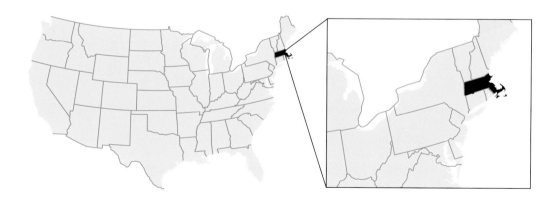

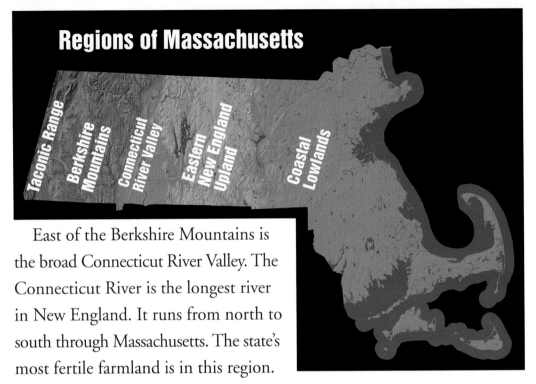

Regions of Massachusetts

Taconic Range

Berkshire Mountains

Connecticut River Valley

Eastern New England Upland

Coastal Lowlands

East of the Berkshire Mountains is the broad Connecticut River Valley. The Connecticut River is the longest river in New England. It runs from north to south through Massachusetts. The state's most fertile farmland is in this region.

In central Massachusetts is the Eastern New England Upland. The land has gently rolling hills, woods, and streams. Many of the state's 3,000 lakes and ponds are found in this region.

The Coastal Lowlands occupy the eastern third of Massachusetts. Flat land or gently rolling hills slope downward toward the Atlantic Ocean. In some areas there are many small lakes, ponds, streams, and swamps. The Charles River is the longest river entirely in the state. It runs through the city of Boston and empties into Boston Harbor.

The Connecticut River runs past fertile Massachusetts farmland.

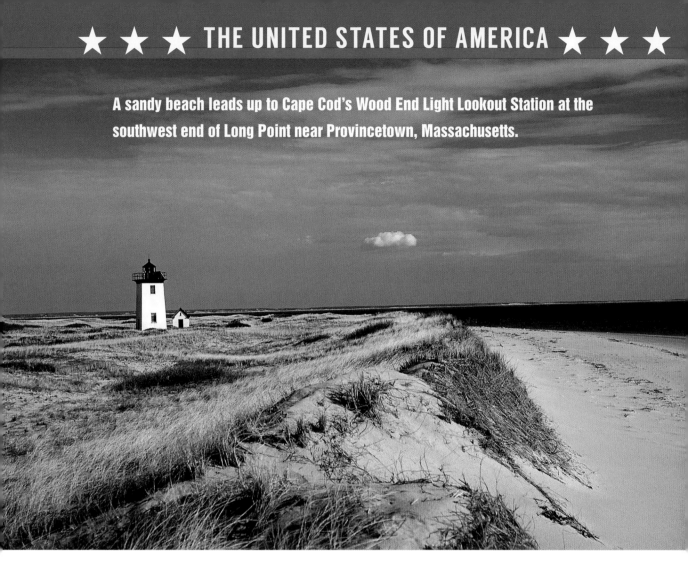

A sandy beach leads up to Cape Cod's Wood End Light Lookout Station at the southwest end of Long Point near Provincetown, Massachusetts.

The shoreline in the north of Massachusetts is rocky. In the southern coast there are windswept sand dunes and salt marshes. There are many bays and coves. The largest include Massachusetts Bay, Cape Cod Bay, and Buzzards Bay.

Cape Cod is in southeastern Massachusetts. It is a 65-mile (105-km) -long peninsula that sticks out like a hook into the Atlantic Ocean. A popular place for sightseers, it has long, sandy beaches, lighthouses, and quaint small towns. Sailing and whale watching are popular activities.

Martha's Vineyard and Nantucket are two large islands south of Cape Cod. They are both popular summer destinations.

GEOGRAPHY

CLIMATE AND
WEATHER

Most of Massachusetts has a humid continental climate. Winters are cold, while summers are hot and humid. The moderating waters of the Atlantic Ocean make the eastern coast of Massachusetts a little less cold in winter and less hot in summer.

Statewide, the average July high temperature is 81°F (27°C). The record high temperature occurred on August 2, 1975, in Chester and New Bedford. Both cities saw the thermometer soar to 107°F (42°C) that day. The average January low temperature is 16°F (-9°C). The state's record low temperature was recorded on January 12, 1981, in Chester, when the mercury sank to -35°F (-37°C).

A hospital worker trudges through deep snow to get to his job in New Bedford.

A spring nor'easter, bringing high winds and driving rain, sends ocean waves blasting against a seawall in Scituate, Massachusetts.

On average, there about 125 days each year when Massachusetts gets rain or snow. The state receives about 48 inches (122 cm) of precipitation each year.

Tornados sometimes strike Massachusetts, but they are rare. More common are large, dangerous storms called nor'easters. They can cause much damage, lashing the state with fierce winds and heavy rains or snow. They usually strike during late autumn and winter. Nor'easters get their name from the northeasterly direction of their winds.

CLIMATE AND WEATHER

PLANTS AND
ANIMALS

Because of its crowded cities and urban areas, many people don't realize that Massachusetts is actually a heavily forested state. More than 3.1 million acres (1.3 million ha), or 62 percent, of the land is covered with trees. Of those forests, 79 percent are privately owned. About 20 percent of the state's forests are protected from development.

Massachusetts forests are filled with deciduous trees that turn color in the fall and shed their leaves in winter. The most common trees include red maple, northern red oak, hickory, hemlock, white pine, and ash. The official state tree is the American elm.

Trees change color in the fall in Willard Brook State Forest.

Bearberry

Water Lily

Wild Columbine

American beachgrass grows 2 to 3 feet (.6 to .9 m) high and is found on coastal beaches and dunes. Bearberry has dark evergreen leaves and bright red berries. It was once a favorite food for bears when they roamed the coastal areas.

Wildflowers throughout Massachusetts make the state's forests and meadows come alive with color. Common wildflowers native to Massachusetts include asters, lilies, orchids, goldenrods, marigolds, and wild red columbines. The state flower is the mayflower.

PLANTS AND ANIMALS

A mother bear looks out from a tree in Barre, Massachusetts, as her cub rests nearby.

White-tailed deer are the most common large mammals spotted in Massachusetts. Black bears were once hunted nearly to extinction in the state, but they have made a comeback thanks to conservation efforts. Most black bears are spotted in the forested hills west of the Connecticut River.

Other mammals often found in Massachusetts include brown bats, beavers, bobcats, coyotes, cottontail rabbits, chipmunks, foxes, moose, fishers, opossums, skunks, squirrels, raccoons, and woodchucks.

Many species of frogs, toads, turtles, salamanders, and snakes live in Massachusetts. Most snakes in the state are nonvenomous, except for two: timber rattlesnakes and northern copperheads. However, it is very rare to encounter either of these reptiles.

Birds often found in Massachusetts include American robins, goldfinches, Baltimore orioles, blue jays, bald eagles, falcons, crows, gulls, sparrows, Canada geese, mockingbirds, cardinals, herons, owls, and woodpeckers. Wild turkeys are recognized by their large tail feathers and noisy gobbling. The official state bird is the black-capped chickadee.

Freshwater fish swimming in the rivers and lakes of Massachusetts include trout, bass, perch, carp, catfish, sunfish, and pickerel. Lurking in the state's coastal waters are haddock, lobsters, shrimp, oysters, and clams. Atlantic cod is the official state fish. Marine mammals spotted offshore include seals and dolphins. There are also several species of whales, including endangered North Atlantic right whales.

A humpback whale breaches at Stellwagen Bank National Marine Sanctuary in Cape Cod, Massachusetts.

HISTORY

The first people to live in present-day Massachusetts were Paleo-Indians. They were the ancestors of today's Native Americans. They arrived in the area after the last of the Ice Age glaciers melted, as early as 12,000 years ago. They hunted with stone spear points. They also fished and grew corn and squash.

As time went on, the Paleo-Indians formed tribes. By the time Europeans arrived in the early 1600s, the Native American tribes included the Mahican, Mohegan, Wampanoag, and Massachuset. The Massachuset people lived near present-day Boston, and it is from them that the state got its name.

On May 15, 1602, English explorer Bartholomew Gosnold sailed into Provincetown Harbor. After viewing huge schools of fish, he named the peninsula "Cape Cod."

Massasoit, the Wampanoag Native American leader, visits the Plymouth Colony in the 1620s.

In 1602, English explorer Bartholomew Gosnold sailed along the shores of Cape Cod. He gave the cape its name because of the plentiful Atlantic codfish found in the ocean there. In 1614, English adventurer Captain John Smith visited the coasts of Maine and Massachusetts and named the region New England.

In 1620, a group of English settlers called Pilgrims came to the New World to find religious freedom. They arrived in Massachusetts aboard a ship named the *Mayflower* and started Plymouth Colony. The Mayflower Compact was a set of laws they used to govern themselves. In time, more Pilgrims arrived and the colony grew.

The Puritans were another group of English people who fled to Massachusetts to find religious freedom. In 1630, they settled Boston and other locations. Together, the settlements were called the Massachusetts Bay Colony. Within just a few years, thousands of colonists, both Puritans and others, occupied the land. Boston grew, and New England's economy boomed.

The Puritans's relationship with Natives Americans was not good. The Puritans expanded westward and took land. The Native Americans fought back in several bloody conflicts, including King Philip's War (1675-1676). The Native Americans were decimated by both warfare and diseases, such as smallpox, for which they had no natural immunity.

King Philip, also known as Metacom, chief of the Wampanoags, led the war against European colonists. In 1675, the colonial village of Brookfield, Massachusetts, was burned. There was much suffering and death on both sides before the colonists won and the fighting ceased in 1676.

A reenactment of the British and Patriot soldiers's conflict at Concord's North Bridge on April 19, 1775. The event sparked the start of the Revolutionary War and became known as the "shot heard 'round the world."

In 1692, Plymouth Colony and a portion of present-day Maine were combined with Massachusetts Bay Colony. The new, larger colony was called the Province of Massachusetts Bay.

Great Britain had a firm grip on its American colonies. Over the next century, the colonists were subjected to many laws and taxes, which they protested were unfair. In 1773, angry citizens boarded three British ships and dumped valuable tea into Boston Harbor. The incident became known as the Boston Tea Party.

The American colonists demanded more freedoms, but Great Britain punished them with more laws and taxes. On April 19, 1775, gunfire broke out between British soldiers and colonists called Minutemen in the towns of Lexington and Concord. The battles marked the beginning of the Revolutionary War (1775-1783).

In 1775, the 13 American colonies united to break free from Great Britain. Massachusetts's troops fought in key battles, including Boston's Battle of Bunker Hill in June 1775. After the siege of Dorchester Heights in 1776, the British army fled Massachusetts.

After the war, Massachusetts played a key part in forming a new national government. On February 6, 1788, it ratified the United States Constitution, becoming the sixth state in the Union. It is officially named the Commonwealth of Massachusetts. "Commonwealth" in this case has the same meaning as "state."

In the early 1800s, agriculture declined as new factories sprang up all over the state. They churned out everything from textiles and shoes, to steam engines and tools. Urban areas like Boston grew rapidly. Railroads, canals, and highways crisscrossed the state, making it easy to transport goods.

A color postcard shows a train passing the Berkshire Hills between Russell and Huntington, Massachusetts.

Civil War officers and men of the 3rd Regiment Massachusetts Heavy Artillery stand ready to protect Washington, DC, at Fort Totten.

In the 1840s and 1850s, the nation was sharply divided over slavery. Massachusetts was a center for abolitionists. Decades before, in the 1780s, it became the first state to outlaw slavery through legal action. When the Civil War (1861-1865) broke out, Massachusetts was among the first states to send Union troops to fight the Southern Confederacy.

In modern times, Massachusetts has replaced many of its factories with high technology, finance, and health care companies. The state keeps its competitive edge, thanks to its highly educated workforce and many world-class universities.

DID YOU KNOW?

- The Great Blizzard of 1888 killed more than 400 people in Massachusetts and neighboring states. From March 11-14, the massive nor'easter dumped more than 50 inches (127 cm) of snow in some Massachusetts locations. High winds caused drifts up to 40 feet (12 m) high. Hundreds of ships sank or ran aground. Major cities, including Boston, were paralyzed for days as residents tried to dig out. It was called "The White Hurricane."

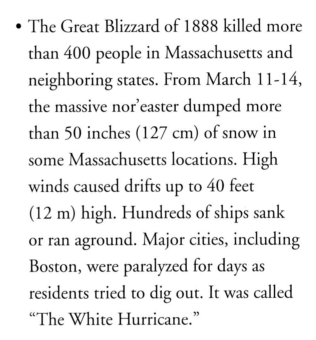

Harvard

MIT

- America's oldest university is in Cambridge, Massachusetts. Harvard University opened in 1636. It is one of the most prestigious universities in the world. Eight United States presidents have Harvard degrees, more than any other university. The renowned Massachusetts Institute of Technology (MIT) is also in Cambridge, across the Charles River from Boston.

• In the early 19th century, whale oil was very valuable. It was used in street lamps and to lubricate machinery. The island of Nantucket, 24 miles (39 km) south of Cape Cod, was a center for whaling. In 1820, a large sperm whale rammed the Nantucket whaling ship *Essex*, sinking it. Most of the crew perished. Author Herman Melville wrote the book *Moby-Dick*, which is based loosely on the *Essex* incident, while living in Massachusetts in 1850.

• The Pilgrims were English people who disagreed with the Church of England. They fled to Holland, but soon decided to start a colony in North America, where they hoped to have religious freedom. A group of about 100 Pilgrims set out in 1620 on the *Mayflower*. The two-month voyage was perilous. They landed at first on Cape Cod, then sailed to Plymouth, where they started their colony. They had few supplies, and sickness took the lives of almost half the colonists during the first year. Helped by the Wampanoag Native Americans, the survivors of Plymouth Colony had a good harvest of crops in 1621. They celebrated with a feast and invited the Wampanoag as guests. It is marked by many as America's first Thanksgiving Day celebration.

DID YOU KNOW?

PEOPLE

John F. Kennedy (1917-1963) was the 35th president of the United States. He served from 1961 until his death by assassination in 1963. Born into a family of wealthy politicians and socialites, Kennedy spent his early  childhood in Brookline, Massachusetts. A Navy war hero during World War II, he later went into politics. He served both in the United States House of Representatives and Senate. After his election as president, Kennedy dealt with many difficulties facing the nation, including the economy, civil rights, the Cold War, the race to put astronauts on the moon, and public service. He famously once said, "Ask not what your country can do for you. Ask what you can do for your country."

Theodor Geisel (1904-1991) is best known as the popular children's book author Dr. Seuss. The name "Seuss" was both Geisel's middle name and his mother's maiden name. He wrote and illustrated such classics as *The Cat in the Hat*, *How the Grinch Stole Christmas*, *Green Eggs and Ham*, and *If I Ran the Zoo*. Over the course of his career, he wrote and illustrated 44 children's books. Geisel was born and grew up in Springfield, Massachusetts.

Alexander Graham Bell (1847-1922) was a scientist whose most famous invention was the telephone. Born in Scotland, he lived for a time in Canada, then moved to Massachusetts to teach deaf students. He set up a laboratory in Boston, where he experimented with adding voice to telegraph lines. In 1876, he invented the telephone. The first spoken words on the new device were to his assistant: "Mr. Watson. Come here. I want to see you." Within a decade, more than 150,000 people in the United States owned telephones.

Susan B. Anthony (1820-1906) was a teacher and social activist. She was an abolitionist in the 1840s and 1850s who wanted an end to slavery. After the Civil War, she devoted her life to women's rights. She gave hundreds of speeches across the country convincing people to give women the right to vote.

She was arrested in 1872 for illegally voting in a presidential election. She was released and fined, but she never paid the $100 fee, telling the judge, "I shall never pay a dollar of your unjust penalty." In 1920, fourteen years after her death, the 19th Amendment to the United States Constitution was passed, giving all women the right to vote. Anthony was born and spent her early childhood in Adams, Massachusetts.

Rocky Marciano (1923-1969) was one of the best boxers of all time. He went undefeated during his professional career. Famous for swarming his opponents with relentless attacks, and for his iron chin, Marciano held the world heavyweight title from 1952-1956, successfully defending it six times. He was born Rocco Francis Marchegiano, but he changed his name so ring announcers could more easily pronounce it. Marciano was born and raised in Brockton, Massachusetts.

Leonard Nimoy (1931-2015) was an actor, film director, author, and photographer. He was most famous for playing Mr. Spock in the original *Star Trek* television series and in several films. He acted in many television shows and movies before starting *Star Trek* in 1966. He became an accomplished film and television director in the 1980s and 1990s. Nimoy was born and raised in Boston, Massachusetts.

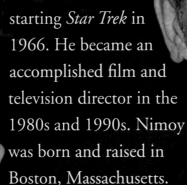

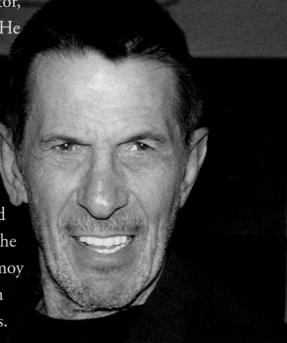

CITIES

Boston is the capital and largest city of Massachusetts. Its population is 655,884. It is the largest city in New England. Founded in 1630, it is one of the nation's oldest cities. Boston's core is a small peninsula that juts into Boston Harbor. Together with its suburbs and surrounding communities, the Greater Boston area is home to nearly five million people. Boston is a world-leading center for education and medicine. Many advanced technology companies are located in the city. Top industries include education, business services, finance, government, and manufacturing. Tourists flock to Boston to see historical attractions along the Freedom Trail (marked with a red brick sidewalk), such as Boston Common, Faneuil Hall, the Old State House, and the USS *Constitution*.

Worcester is the second-biggest city in Massachusetts. Its population is 183,016. Worcester is in the central part of the state, which led to its nickname as the "Heart of the Commonwealth." Like many cities in Massachusetts, Worcester started as a farming center, then shifted to industry. Good highways and railroads helped the city become a major distribution center for products sold in New England. Today, biotechnology and other high-tech industries are important to the city's economy. Other big employers are health care, insurance, and education. The city boasts more than 1,200 acres (486 ha) of parkland.

Springfield is the third-largest city in Massachusetts. Its population is 153,991. It is located along the banks of the Connecticut River in south-central Massachusetts. It was founded in 1636 as a fur-trading post. The city's biggest industries are transportation, health care, manufacturing, and tourism. There are 25 universities and colleges in the city and nearby. High-tech manufacturing brings in thousands of jobs. Springfield is home to the Basketball Hall of Fame. The game was invented in 1891 by Springfield teacher and coach James Naismith. Other Springfield attractions include the Dr. Seuss National Memorial Sculpture Garden, the Michele and Donald D'Amour Museum of Fine Arts, and the Springfield Science Museum.

Lowell is located in northeastern Massachusetts, near the border of New Hampshire. It is the fourth-largest city in Massachusetts. Its population is 109,945. In the 1820s, Lowell became a textile-milling powerhouse as it rode the first wave of the Industrial Revolution. By the 1850s, it was the largest manufacturing center in the country. Today, Lowell continues to be a manufacturing city, but its economy also depends on health care, telecommunications, education, and tourism. The New England Quilt Museum includes a library, classrooms, and galleries that show off the history and art of quiltmaking. The Lowell National Historical Park preserves several mills and other 19th century buildings highlighting the city's textile-making heritage.

TRANSPORTATION

Massachusetts has five major seaports. The biggest is the Port of Boston. Large cargo ships can dock here, as well as passenger cruise ships. The dock's activity supports more than 50,000 jobs and contributes more than $4.6 billion to the economy. Because it is the closest United States port to Europe, many imported automobiles pass through here.

The busiest airport in Massachusetts is Boston's Logan International Airport. Named after Boston native General Edward Lawrence Logan, the airport has six runways and serves more than 33 million passengers yearly. Other busy Massachusetts airports are located in Nantucket, Hyannis, Worcester, Martha's Vineyard, New Bedford, and Provincetown. There are also dozens of smaller airports scattered throughout the state.

A large container ship is unloaded at the Port of Boston.

The Thomas P. O'Neill Jr. Tunnel runs underneath the downtown area of Boston. The tunnel was completed in 2006. It is named after "Tip" O'Neill, a member of the House of Representatives for 34 years.

Massachusetts has 36,370 miles (58,532 km) of public roadways. Interstate 90, also called the Massachusetts Turnpike, enters the western side of the state and travels east all the way to Boston. Measuring 136 miles (219 km), it is the longest interstate in Massachusetts.

"The Big Dig" is the nickname of a huge construction project that tunneled under Boston to ease traffic through the city. The 3.5-mile (5.6 km) tunnel is officially named the Thomas P. O'Neill Jr. Tunnel, in honor of the long-serving United States congressman from Massachusetts.

There are 973 miles (1,566 km) of freight railroad lines crisscrossing Massachusetts. Amtrak also operates several lines of passenger trains.

NATURAL
RESOURCES

About 62 percent, or 3.1 million acres (1.3 million ha) of Massachusetts is covered by forestland, but most of that is privately owned. Some trees in the western part of the state are harvested. Red oak, sugar maple, and ash are prized hardwoods for making cabinetry. For the state's other lumber needs, such as for making paper and wood products, about 98 percent of the trees needed are imported from other states.

The seafood industry in Massachusetts supports more than 107,000 jobs and adds approximately $8.5 billion to the economy. The most important commercial fishing catches include lobster, cod, herring, pollock, and sea scallops.

Valuable non-metallic minerals mined from Massachusetts include clay, lime, marble, quartz, granite, limestone, and sandstone.

A commercial fishing boat hauls in a net filled with yellowtail flounder and Atlantic cod from Stellwagen Bank at the mouth of Massachusetts Bay.

A farmer uses a water picker to harvest the first cranberries of the season at a bog in Marion, Massachusetts. The cranberries will be used to make juice.

In the colonial times of the 17th and 18th centuries, fishing and farming strengthened Massachusetts. The state's economy has now changed, but farming is still important. Today, agriculture is located mainly in the southeastern and western parts of the state, especially along the fertile river valleys. There are about 7,800 farms operating in Massachusetts. The most valuable products are greenhouse and nursery plants, followed by fruits and berries. Massachusetts is one of the top producers of cranberries in the nation. There are many cranberry farms in southeast Massachusetts. Other important farm products include dairy, cattle, hogs, hay, apples, potatoes, peaches, and sweet corn.

NATURAL RESOURCES

INDUSTRY

The overall economy of Massachusetts is strong. Residents have a higher household income than most other states. Workers are highly educated and have jobs in industries that are resistant to economic hard times. Communications, information technology, and biotechnology are all vital industries. Financial services, computer hardware manufacturing, health care, and tourism are also important.

There are hundreds of biotechnology companies in Massachusetts. They use living organisms to make medicines such as life-saving cancer drugs. They also find new ways to grow crops.

Massachusetts's technology companies depend on a highly educated workforce. The state is home to some of the oldest and most prestigious universities in the world. They include Harvard University, Massachusetts Institute of Technology, Brandeis University, Tufts University, and Wellesley College.

A biotechnology student works at a lab at the University of Massachusetts-Dartmouth campus. Biotechnology is an important industry in the state.

Massachusetts beaches and lighthouses are popular tourist attractions.

In the 19th century, Massachusetts was a powerful manufacturing center. Today, manufacturing is a smaller part of the state economy, but it is still important. Some of the many products made in Massachusetts factories include electronics and computers, machinery, scientific instruments, printed goods, leather products, and fabricated metals.

Tourism supports more than 129,000 jobs in the state. Visitors enjoy the many historical sites, especially in the Boston area. Cape Cod is known for its sandy beaches, legendary seafood, and whale watching. The Berkshire Mountains are also a popular getaway destination.

INDUSTRY

SPORTS

The New England Patriots play in the National Football League. They have won the Super Bowl four times. The Boston Red Sox are a Major League Baseball team. They have played in Fenway Park since 1912. It is the oldest ballpark in Major League Baseball. The Red Sox have won eight World Series championships.

The Boston Bruins skate in the National Hockey League. Founded in 1924, the team has won the Stanley Cup championship title six times. The Boston Celtics compete in the National Basketball Association. Their well-known "Lucky the Leprechaun" mascot is a tip o' the hat to Boston's many Irish immigrants. The team has won 17 NBA championships. The Naismith Memorial Basketball Hall of Fame is in Springfield, Massachusetts.

The New England Revolution is a Major League Soccer team. The "Revs" won the U.S. Open Cup in 2007, and have reached the MLS Cup finals five times.

There are a large number of other professional teams in Massachusetts, representing many different sports. They include lacrosse, rugby, tennis, and even paintball. College sports are also very popular.

International **Volleyball** HALL *of* FAME

Volleyball was invented in Massachusetts in 1895 by William Morgan. The International Volleyball Hall of Fame is in Holyoke, Massachusetts.

Every year since 1897, thousands of athletes have run through the streets of Boston competing in the world-famous Boston Marathon. The event attracts about half a million spectators each year.

Athletes compete in the Boston Marathon. The race starts in the town of Hopkinton and finishes near Boston's John Hancock Tower in Copley Square.

SPORTS

ENTERTAINMENT

The Boston Symphony Orchestra has been playing classical music since 1881. The Boston Pops Orchestra plays light classical and popular music. Other Massachusetts orchestras include the Springfield Symphony Orchestra and the Cape Cod Symphony Orchestra in Barnstable.

Boston is also home to the Boston Ballet and the Boston Lyric Opera. There are several world-class theater companies. The Boston Museum of Fine Arts, with its 500,000 works of art, is one of the largest and most-visited museums in the United States.

Massachusetts is rich in historical buildings and museums. Many of the sites from the American Revolution have been preserved or restored. In Boston Harbor, visitors can tour the USS *Constitution*. Dubbed "Old Ironsides," this three-masted frigate is famous for defeating several British warships during the War of 1812.

The popular Boston Pops Orchestra plays for the Fourth of July celebration in Boston, Massachusetts.

The Franklin Park Zoo has many animal species, including lions and gorillas.

The Franklin Park Zoo is in Boston. Founded in 1912, it houses many animal species, including tigers, lions, giraffes, and gorillas.

Boston Common is a 50-acre (20 ha) park in downtown Boston. Founded in 1634, it is the oldest city park in the country. Next door is Boston Public Garden, with flower beds and a large lake in the center. It is famously the setting for the beloved children's book *Make Way for Ducklings* by Robert McCloskey.

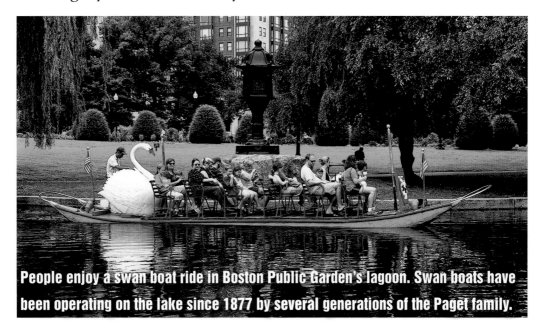

People enjoy a swan boat ride in Boston Public Garden's lagoon. Swan boats have been operating on the lake since 1877 by several generations of the Paget family.

TIMELINE

10,000 BC—Massachusetts is first settled by Paleo-Indians, prehistoric ancestors of today's Native Americans.

1602—Bartholomew Gosnold sails along the shores of Cape Cod.

1614—John Smith visits the coast of Maine and Massachusetts and names the region New England.

1620—Pilgrims land in Massachusetts and start Plymouth Colony.

1621—The Pilgrims host one of America's first Thanksgiving Day celebrations.

1630—Puritans land at Boston and start the Massachusetts Bay Colony.

1675—King Philip's War begins. There is bloody fighting between colonists and Native Americans.

1692—Colonies merge into the Province of Massachusetts Bay.

1773—Angry citizens board three British ships and dump valuable tea into Boston Harbor. This later becomes known as the Boston Tea Party.

1775—The Battles of Lexington and Concord mark the beginning of the Revolutionary War and America's fight for independence.

1788—Massachusetts becomes the sixth state in the Union.

1861—The Civil War begins. Massachusetts is among the first states to send troops to fight for the Union.

1876—Massachusetts becomes a technology leader with the invention of the telephone by Alexander Graham Bell.

1961—Massachusetts native John F. Kennedy becomes the youngest person in American history to serve as president.

2013—Two terrorist bombs explode near the Boston Marathon's finish line, killing three and injuring hundreds. The terrorists are found and brought to justice.

2015—The New England Patriots win the National Football League's Super Bowl championship for the fourth time in 14 years.

GLOSSARY

ABOLITIONIST

A person who favors the banning of an activity, such as slavery or the death penalty.

AMERICAN REVOLUTION

The war fought between the American colonies and Great Britain from 1775-1783. It is also known as the War of Independence or the Revolutionary War.

BIOTECHNOLOGY

The use of living organisms to make products, such as drugs or hormones.

CIVIL WAR

The war fought between America's Northern and Southern states from 1861-1865. The Southern states were for slavery. They wanted to start their own country. Northern states fought against slavery and a division of the country.

COLD WAR

A period of tension and hostility between the United States and its allies versus the Soviet Union, China, and their allies after World War II. The Cold War ended after the Soviet Union collapsed in 1991.

COLONY

A colony is the establishment of a settlement in a new location. It is often ruled by another country.

COMMONWEALTH

An old word for a government formed to promote the common good of the people. Massachusetts declares itself a commonwealth, but is considered a state by the United States Constitution.

INDUSTRIAL REVOLUTION

A period of time starting in the late 1700s when machines began taking over many types of work that before had been done by hand.

MINUTEMEN

Massachusetts citizen-soldiers of the American Revolution. Mainly farmers and shopkeepers, they trained themselves in military tactics. They were ready at a moment's notice to fight against British troops.

NEW ENGLAND

An area in the northeastern United States consisting of six states. It includes Maine, New Hampshire, Massachusetts, Rhode Island, Vermont, and Connecticut.

NOR'EASTER

A large storm that forms when warm air over the Atlantic Ocean clashes with cold Arctic air blown in from Canada. Nor'easters get their name from the northeasterly direction of their winds. They can be very destructive, but are usually less dangerous than tropical hurricanes.

PALEO-INDIANS

Prehistoric ancestors of today's Native Americans.

PILGRIMS

A group of English men, women, and children who fled their country because the government hated their ideas about religion and worship.

INDEX